Where Green Meets Blue

poems by

Elizabeth Robin

Finishing Line Press
Georgetown, Kentucky

Where Green Meets Blue

This book is dedicated to the many talents who guide me in the craft:

Island Writers' Network for its continued support and incisive critique, island artist Mira Scott for her painting, Rice Fields by Moonlight, the marvelous poets of Truchas, 2016—

And always, to Brandon, Lauren and Amanda, my loves.

And to George, whose voice still guides me in this crazy whereafter. Love, stitched inside.

Copyright © 2018 by Elizabeth Robin
ISBN 978-1-63534-487-5 First Edition
All rights reserved under International and Pan-American Copyright Conventions.
No part of this book may be reproduced in any manner whatsoever without written permission from the publisher, except in the case of brief quotations embodied in critical articles and reviews.

ACKNOWLEDGMENTS

Thank you to the following publications in which these poems first appeared, some in slightly different form:

"The Lowcountry Path" *The Breeze*, January 2015
"Solo" *Skinny Poetry Journal*, June 23, 2016
"A Split Screen World" *i am not a silent poet*, October 30, 2015
"A Pantoum of Perfect Symmetry" *The Fourth River* [Climate Change Insert], Spring 2016
"Inaction # Distraction" *Curly Mind*, April 17, 2016
"Whereafter," "A Maze" and "The Price of Coral" *Ebb and Flow*, a collection from the Island Writers' Network, 2017
"Carolina in Gold, Silver and Brown" *Good Juju Review* March, 2018

Publisher: Leah Maines
Editor: Christen Kincaid
Cover Art: Danielle Klim
Author Photo: Cara Donoghue
Cover Design: Elizabeth Maines McCleavy

Printed in the USA on acid-free paper.
Order online: www.finishinglinepress.com
also available on amazon.com

Author inquiries and mail orders:
Finishing Line Press
P. O. Box 1626
Georgetown, Kentucky 40324
U. S. A.

Table of Contents

The Lowcountry Path 1
Spin-Out 2
Stand By 3
One Daffodil 4
Solo, A Skinny Poem 6
Whereafter 7
Lean Out 8
At the Arco Lounge 9
Dear David 10
Maybe, Baby 12
God's Plan 13
It's Raining Mice 14
A Split Screen World 15
A Maze 19
A Holocaust Remembrance 20
Double-Dipping 22
Opaque Memories 23
The Price of Coral 24
Carolina Gold, Silver and Brown 25
Fair Trade, A Skinny Poem 27
A Pantoum of Perfect Symmetry 28
Inaction # Distraction 30
Lasagna for One 31
Exceptionalism 32
See-Saw 33

The Lowcountry Path

some roll by, or strut; others trot
wrapped in oblivion, unmoving
some blast through like leafblowers
scattering us off their narrow paths

but the wisest saunter, breathe in
listen as the woodpecker knocks
watch the gator and gray heron
sunning in side by side detente

or catch another's eye, stop, and trade
wonderful stories of astonishing pasts
hard-fought wisdoms that warm and teach

avoid the passersby, frozen in mad
scurries and take the prettier
path at a proper lowcountry pace

Spin-Out

velvet ropes slither across my skin
what should feel soft, erotic
foreshadows a turbulent ride

a lopsided caricature in iron
painted white, disappears into butter
churning   inside a bee's foot
that thumps to the beat   of a ska   cha-cha

like wire-wrapped sculpting
each strand twists and bends
until a form emerges
Bird Nesting. Lovers Entwined.

pieces—iron, wire, velvet—spin
fragmented mementoes that boil
       drift, sway   out
                    up and   away from meaning
    fly

a heart agonizes, the sad supplicant
awaiting some exercise in creation

Stand By

i feel each singular skin cell pressing inward
underwater, not drowning, but unable to breathe

thick rain-filled clouds speed across the sky
doom lurks. forecasts call for deluge
pockmarked radar warns of tornadoes
ahead i see a twisted path, dainty
plodding through caring betrayals

how can i explain? no one's home
i stare into the storm
watch limbs sway and drop
longing to become the bark
that squirrels scurry along
that redstarts cling to
that rain kisses

the woodpecker ravishes
and the osprey nests inside
until, somehow, my roots gnarl
back into the firm, rich earth

One Daffodil

no gardens bloom in Bay Head that spring

surviving structures instead display
an empty swathe of sand and debris

crepe myrtle and lavender and boxwoods and cherry trees
lynchpins that hold the dunes in place
                      vanished

chunks of errant concrete, broken glass, twisted metal
garnish blackened roots and brown brush

a place rubbish comes to die

and yet, a fragment of yellow, a slender green stem
pushes from that rubble

one daffodil, alive and well
one bulb that somehow
came to rest
            took root
                        found nourishment

south of Bay Head most of Mantoloking disappeared
steel beams holding a bridge buckled
in Seaside, the iconic latticed iron rollercoaster
twisted, snapped, swept away in minutes

mayhem can be shockingly democratic

    the tensile strength underpinning
           a house
                     or bridge
fails

it lacks the mettle of one daffodil

there it sits, the sole survivor
one fragile flower, a whisper of what was
sprung from the wreckage of Sandy

Solo
    A skinny poem . . .

bluejays squawk a tango, as if their duende dies in the downpour

mourning

past

rains,

souls

mourning

futures

screamed

empty,

mourning

as if bluejays pour a tango down duendes, and their squawks die

Whereafter

he strokes my back the way he did just before
he'd fold me in his warmth. scalp tingling,
i sit on the stump of a ponderosa pine,
the sky as cerulean as the ocean we swam
on our honeymoon. i hear the waves
through the trees, lapping some magic shore.

i crouch, hunched and small under that blue.
i sense his fingers flutter through my hair,
smell that vanilla musk, wonder: tree bark?
his skin? and tears dampen dry tinder.

the wind sways the treetops
not our island shore. a breeze
touches me the way he did.
i watch the pinetops and calm.

where green meets blue
i remember, he loved that view

stitched into the seam
of this whereafter
memories seep through

Lean Out

not for long . . .
an island expression
when trees or people
lean out of life

press a foot against
some pines and find
air pockets

time to dismantle
scale with rope
and hobnail boots

shred in chippers

did he deserve
a piecemeal ending?
the neighborhood tragedy
trodding the boards?

i'm left with the stump
lifeless, flat, unmoved

oversized hands
wise eyes
and a rumbling humor

At the Arco Lounge

i sit in solitude, surrounded
looped into the motown track
dancing lanterns light the ceiling

my eyes gravitate to a black and white
perm woman in cat's eye glasses
kissing a parakeet. her ecstasy
draws me back again and again

blown out of proportion
she looms above table twenty
a portent perhaps, of joy
even as gray skies wet passersby
a constant scrim when stuck
in the arco lounge in the rain

the buzz of conversation mutes
smokey and michael and gladys
as coffee shop companions sipping
hot chocolate and newsfeeds pause
settle into the cover and watch

she glows in one simple moment
i stare bemused, lost in questions
and the comfortable routine
of lonely thoughts
unvoiced at a table for one

Dear David

you caught my eye very young
created an impossible standard
    of male beauty
the lean, long-backed proportions
the tapered, muscular thighs
the bulging, shapely calves
big, capable hands

but when i measured that pristine, marble chest
assessed sculpted abs, that beautifully large
    missing fig leaf
the serene unassuming way you looked out upon the world
there, at age eight, you had me

i searched for years to find you
but the nose or a calf or that burgeoning sex
never quite fit the model

what perfect renaissance man
did Michelangelo find, and how?
surely my David
had been replicated
    somewhere

can flesh improve on marble?

the discovery of tactile warmth
dimples and moles and birthmarks
    tickle spots
years thinning or fattening
into wrinkles and scars

a quiet ecstasy, David

while you remain coldly perfect
only needing occasional scrubbing
from the smudges of Florentine air
at five-hundred some years old
your agelessness taunts
how i've changed in far fewer years

i see you differently, now
an ideal somehow imperfect
endlessly on display, rigid
missing comfortable wear
the joy of familiarity
the reality of mortality

you do endure, dear David
offer idolatry to unending little girls

but flesh is so much better than marble

Maybe, Baby

Maybe, if the hot oil man from Charleston
looked more like George Clooney
and less like Fred Mertz
i might want to hear his description
of what he'll do to my g-spot
two sentences into our first email exchange

Maybe, if match-dot-com was less like the process
of picking a sticker off cheap merchandise
torn bit by bit into what i can't be
and more like that turtle that trespasses
on my patio and sticks out his little neck

Maybe then, my fur-covered palate
every taste reeking musk, might savor
the randomness of possibility

Maybe the difference between confidence and arrogance
correlates to yes and no answers, and the prestige
collected in junk mail, matches today's winks

Maybe grief requires no ziplock bag to stay fresh

Maybe, attack worms will distract me today
or maybe, i'll catch and release a frog
or sell a haunted house on a murderer's street

And maybe, when I just can't open
that jar, i'll look for a new man

God's Plan

In the trial of counting blessings
what's left, after the storm?

Broken pipes.
Watersoaked baggage.
Snakes in the wall.

One home, hole-punched
next to another, untouched.

Haves and have-nots.

Must we always sift
into winners and losers?

Like tall pines that twist and snap,
nature's radical pruning tests.

Enter the needy predators
and trust dissolves
with the treeline.

We market a chance
escape as God's touch—

No one exudes self
righteousness better
than the faithful.

It's Raining Mice

trouble and joy
often ripple in
flipside tidal fronts
rumbling away silence

droppings hint
at some small invasion
a glimpsed scurry
unsettles perspective

Is there something out there, waiting?

one day, of course,
holes poke through the walls
that keep us safe and separated
from all that's wild and untenable

suddenly, the world is raining mice
eating through any sense
we can remain clean
and free of vermin

Set traps! Plant poison!
a game that feeds a bitter truth

it's always
               always
                              raining
mice
      mice
            mice
                  mice
                        mice

A Split Screen World

Live from Las Vegas!
Live from the Vatican!
banners of a bifurcated news . . .

Ladies and gentlemen! On the left we have
Domestic Product Line Goddess!
Miracle of the Wall Street Boom!
Exclusive contract with Macy's!
JC Penney's! And . . . Home Depot!

On the right we have . . . White Smoke!
A packed Vatican Square!
Only the obelisk visible amongst
praying, praising, palavering masses.
A world awaits the newest Roman emperor
in custom-made red Gucci slip-ons—
dancing shoes for hits like "Pedophilia Exposé"

These scenes pull away
from garage-door windows
frames to an unfolding drama:
a sliver of water, disturbs into a line
monochromatic bubbles speeding
toward a turtle paddling, diving
oblivious to an audience wondering
Do alligators eat turtles?
Will the turtle see him in time?

seven rectangles create an HD multiplex
lining the dead space between the tense
encounter and the gym ceiling, like a bar code
one swipes to purchase an unedited view

channeling seven visions of a split-screen world
CNN remains on smoke. a ticker tape bottom-scrolls
a booming market surge and streaming headlines
Austrian skier crashes during Super G . . .
Congressman downplays role wars have had on the nation's debt

read this and miss the gator lunge
snap the turtle up, only to spit it out
a morsel needing too much ambition
miss the stark white egret sweeping
across the murky water, wings floating
in a lazy arc of slender grace. miss the pudgy
bluejay dart, peck, swoop at the trespassing
cardinal, a swirl of sky-n-scarlet punctuating
layered olive, avocado, and bottle greens
lush lagoon palmettos, crape myrtles, bamboo

Everything in life is a choice.

in Las Vegas one felon among many
signs and breaks contracts
to spectacular applause, a star
of the news circuit. unashamed.

in Rome one empire, rich and well
insulated, expands its corporation
with reproductive dictates worldwide.
Choose life. Tax free.

Fox remains on smoke, a ticker tape bottom-scrolls
a booming market surge and streaming headlines
Judge strikes down NYC ban on sugary drinks . . .
mayor appeals . . .
Pundit rejoices on behalf of "liberty loving soda drinkers" . . .

i could watch the screens all day. some do.
Everything in life is a choice.

or, i could stroll the stretched-wide flat sands
watch comedic interplay in a lowcountry
lab's fruitless sandpiper chase
marvel the revelations of an ebbing tide:
jellyfish larger than basketballs, long tentacles menacing still,
sand dollars clinging, bared conchs, glimmering shells
dolphins slipping along in happy splashes below pelican vees,
a sudden, singular dive-pause-waterplume, its chandelle return

each vista offers its own morality play
what makes news here, does not find
its way into the network divide

nor does *Moms Take the Hill*
who that same day the screens did not witness
flooding the Capital with paper dolls
a cyberbarrage from more than 80,000 women
paper doll strings, eight in each

the eight children killed every day
by gun violence
in America

but not on Fox, or CNN, or MSNBC
... not anywhere

rather, a TV chef whips up her latest pork chop
in her slimmed-down self: that made news

As the World Turns into the tedious amorality
of a daytime saga, one affair at a time
screens, split in their mindless busywork
laud the unscrupulous corporate queen

anticipate the Pope's clandestine election
elevate numerical shifts to oracle status
push headlines that distract or numb

look at the sweeping tides that sway salt marsh grass
look at the majestic ancient oak dripping mossy veils
watch the canine melodrama of mix and mingle
watch the slow blur-by of chickadee acrobatics
and osprey swoops, stopping to bask in a sun-soaked
patch blooming yellows and magentas and lavenders

i could watch the screens all day. some do.
a flickering worship of what they empower
a junta bystander, the man of God
a deal-welching inside trader, the woman of Commerce

Justify. Rationalize. Excuse.

bee colonies collapse in startling mystery
wetlands disappear, wells salinize
epic alterations: ice shelves melt, species dwindle

young lives snuffed out
every day
eight

our screens do not split for this news

what cannot live in America
who dies in America
threatens the survival of Americans
does not live in our split screen world

Everything in life is a choice.

Choose life.

A Maze

i walked the labyrinth today
after staring at cathedral ceilings

they say it mimics the twists and turns
life offers. but its stones are smooth
the path clear, each curve mapped

no choices
no disasters
no tears

just the mild joy
of a childish meander

persist, and find
life's center

a mythical cliche
a fenced limbo
tied to dust and ashes

as in many paths
everyone arrives

A Holocaust Remembrance

> On April 16, 2007 a 76-year-old Virginia Polytechnic Institute professor heard gunfire and blocked the door of his Norris Hall classroom to allow his students to jump to safety. A gunman forced his way into the classroom and killed the professor and one student. Twenty-two students survived. Ensuing news coverage reported he originally came from Romania, where he survived the Holocaust. His death occurred on the date Yom Hashoah fell that year.

Dear Liviu Librescu, engineering science and math lecturer,
I have a few questions . . .

What did you think when you heard him outside
pushed closed the door
blocked the gunman's path
yelled, *Save yourselves!*
Jump out the windows!
Go—just go!

I can imagine the scene:
instant chaos, rapid heart rate
bedlam—but this time
you're not a kid
you're in charge

Did you flash back to those days
when you were eleven or twelve
and they wreaked havoc on your young life?

Did you wonder
Again?

What made you propel
yourself between them?

Did you even get your morning coffee?

In those fleeting seconds
what was on your mind?
I'm old, they're young...
I'm their teacher, I have to protect them...
I won't just watch the horror...
I can't stand for this: Never Again!

just two little words
that never come true

How could they jump, desert you?

How could they not, and betray your dying wish?

How ironic—
that just doesn't cut it.

How tragic—
that just isn't true.

That you show us all to face down horror
a lesson learned so long ago
how magnificent

Again

Double-Dipping

white-robed figures stride single-file
into a roiling ocean
waves a rolling conveyor belt

she finds attending to the wedding at hand
impossible as the drama unfolds at Beach Two

will they find Jesus, sucked out by the magnetic rips?
will they end face-down, pounded by an anvil wave?

each baptism offers a new wrinkle to the plotline
one smoothly dips, lifts, strides back out
as though nature has no power

the next seems God's response to such hauteur
both priest and parishioner, swept into the eddy
tossed about like nervous thoroughbreds before the gate
as others rush in, attempt a grab-and-pull rescue

yet more find in the hand of God swift retribution
slammed to the sand and surf, wave after wave
pressing in the message: saving carries costs

she and her companion cannot suppress guffaws
at each dramatic entrance—and exit—

Shakespeare would be rapt—a study in wave
physics and random chaos too distant
for a soundtrack, pantomimes pure theater

Opaque Memories

in the labyrinth of a calcified brain
repose revelations, if only some map
can retrieve the itinerary

if tapping into bungholes flowing facts
brought back memories

only what haunts, ghosts that whisper
warnings that rampage through a head
steaming a blank imagination
ethereal meanderings on the edge of recovering
if only i could

but the frost coats each synapse
locking out concrete
i anger, lash out, sleep
watch fresh reruns, almost know
hear a voice, but the face?

i absorb their disappointment
sink in their despair

my life is so present
each day so fresh and new
it feels stale
if only i knew why

when were you born and where?
did you have any pets growing up?
heroes? vacations? each day seething
through another quiz show
without the buzzer

The Price of Coral

Turn white and die!
such a catchy slogan might amuse
if stark truths awakened
any sense of alarm or purpose
but we flock to watch our victims

four thousand years in the making
the gentle rainforests of the sea
live in elegant algal symbiosis
inhabit a sliver and foster an ocean
one marvel spotted even in space

would that coral turned its stinging cells
on us, squeezed us in its tentacle rings

a snorkeling wonder teemed diversity
now but a pale discordant shadow
the ocean bottoms turn white
and we deny, deny, deny, swimming
one stroke closer to a color-free world

a licensed vendor stops by with a case
of cheap beads and coral bracelets
pinks and reds—no white here
even our jewels reek of murder

Carolina Gold, Silver and Brown
Inspired by Mira Scott's painting Rice Fields by Moonlight

native cypress and gum guard the swamp
towers fastened to a root maze
home to water moc and gator
the frog chorus fills the fecund night
moonlight filters through spanish moss

history changes in obscurity
as one seedling bag shrouded in myth
arrives: a gift? a discovery? records
etch in the ambiguous tide's flow
the moon watches over a virgin rice field

soon a door of no return opens west
from a dungeon seeds and slaves flow
across the middle passage in a stream
of death and disease and destiny
the idyllic antebellum builds
on brown backs and brains
the impassive moon shines silvery and unaware

lighting a swath of carolina gold
swaying green and ocher as soft tides
flood in, ebb out—the paddies mute
a deeper history than breeze and glitter on the water
a swollen silver moon hangs low, feathered in night clouds

homeland betrayal sends millions through that door
to empires for few, piled on the bodies of many
enslaved to cash crops forging Georgetown and Charleston
but souls sullied discarding humanity pay a price
and the moon glows golden, a benign warden

West African know-how and back-breaking clearing
open fields and the canals to flood them
move earth—enough to fill three Cheops
so Carolina gold pays taxes for belles and gents
while a moon rises above underground railroads

the irony rich, post-bellum gullahs
cultivate small plots of rice and eat well
dum spiro spero—while i breathe, i hope
white hoods bring freedom, and the moonlight
spots five-hundred masked men invading
a union county jail to lynch eight—
hope jim crow only limits where to eat
and who to adopt, hope to end corridors
of shame and mother emanuels, good ol' boy
networks that pave roads and lay
sewer lines serving only some
as the moon looms in contemplation

enslavement happens now in minimum wages
right to work jobs, tourists but no housing or buses
boutique rice
prison segregation and a pretense
stars and bars mean freedom
but while i breathe i hope the maddening
impassive moon beams a luster unchanged

Fair Trade
Another Skinny Poem

specially designed locked chests held exotic spices from the east:

treasures

ex   acted

ex   tracted

im   pacted

treasures

ta   sted

lam   basted

de   se   cra   sted

treasures

held and locked. chests from the east spice designs (especially for exotics)

A Pantoum of Perfect Symmetry

At the Bedruthian Steps during King Tide
one daughter alongside, the other refusing
water roars out, baring a mile or more of sand
at the scope of an ocean's power, they marvel.

With one daughter alongside, the other refusing
like a dried-up scab scratched into rebleeding
cliffs erode; at the ocean's power, they marvel
as the tide turns and resubmerges steps and cliffs.

And like a dried-up scab scratched into rebleeding,
temperatures rise, melting shorelines to Ohio;
the tide turns, resubmerges all steps and cliffs—
what perfect symmetry in nature's verdicts!

While temperatures rise, melting shorelines to Ohio,
we wipe out large predators, and prey eat all scrub;
such perfect symmetry in nature's verdicts—
voilá: landslides erase entire neighborhoods . . .

We wipe out large predators and prey eat all scrub,
suck an aquifer dry, and sinkholes swallow us whole;
landslides erase a neighborhood—voilá, symmetry:
frack inside rocky cracks, and Earth shakes us down.

So we suck an aquifer dry, and sinkholes swallow us
because we waste water, says an eight year old boy;
frack inside rocky cracks, and Earth shakes us down—
we'd better plan on Mars, so we have somewhere.

Because we kill, says this eight year old boy,
even frogs and monarchs and bees and trees,
we'd better plan on Mars, so we have somewhere;
and she: brilliant, Oh Pioneers, let's ruin Mars . . .

Even frogs and monarchs and bees and trees?
cries one daughter, enthralled by Carnewas Cliffs;
she responds, and then let's ruin Mars,
still amazed by the Bedruthian Steps during King Tide.

Inaction # Distraction

delightful wisdom pulls from tightly folded cookies
unblocked, on paper strips inscribed by ancients

Trust in the love of a handsome stranger—
The mask hides the truth—
Wherever joy lives, so do children—

fortunes tied into some thin belief
in the magical property of just-write phrasing

now a typographic charm
a pound sign—four crosses—the sorcerer's hashtag
thrown before a flippant remark or clever slogan
signals our bit for social justice is done

#BringBackOurGirls
#SandyHookPromise

we create anonymous support groups
#amwriting #shoutyourabortion
or nonsensical holidays
#firstlinefriday #throwbackthursday
catchy campaigns to *#makeamericagreatagain*
affirmed by hits and retweets in headline news
where viral tawdry gossip floats
on the global intercom, vessel overflowing
with prurient repetition, spam and food porn
hash into nothingness, and after two years
two-hundred seventy-six missing girls fade
under their hashtag, and the murder of twenty
first-graders loses the pound-key promise
drowned by a Kardashian baby or Minister's affair

#payattention #integrityisyourfortune

Lasagna for One

Everyday rituals strip loneliness bare
measured in plates and glasses
repeating leftovers and empty dishwashers.

That picked over roast chicken
a reminder that no one's here.

How to ladle a pot of soup into one bowl?
A hearty stew onto a single plate?

Trivial challenges in a world of crazed bomb
throwers, wild shooters and starving, homeless
moms trudging, babies strapped to their backs.

Locked into meager, petty routine
upended by newsfeed tragedies
unable to lift a spoon
or calculate construction
of one pancake
                        i freeze

Exceptionalism

Funneling her car through a gauntlet
of orange phosphorescent barrels
she navigates a reconstructing world
less green, less alive, less interesting.

She wonders where her brother's ashes are scattered.
She wonders why they keep this from her.
She wonders when she lost consequence.

She wonders, again, what tables Jesus
would overturn at their fact-bending
complex web of wild fabrications.

Yet, they dot every tee, and every eye crosses
to a bridge without a nose, a limbo of lost
connections carved away by their fiction.

We win when we leap to faith. Then, we're
carmelized like boardwalk onions, ground
in angus elk or bison. We build our own truth
like that game of trust, believing if we let go
someone will catch us before we crack our skulls.

See-Saw
> *A poem of semordnilap . . .*

when forward goes backward
so reverse progresses, i stop

and *rail* against the *liar*
reward instead the *drawer*
sketching the *dray* in the *yard*

flog evil with *live golf*
throw *serif* into the *fires*
get *faced* on laced *decaf*

in *part* this direction's a *trap*
a *reflip* meant to *pilfer* souls

but only a lone *wolf* stems their *flow*

the great *raja* whose mind's *ajar*
takes the *tram* to rose compass *mart*
where the past meets the present
and direction becomes art

when the *spacer recaps* the *rif* of a *fir*
and a *rater retars* a roof 'til she's sure
the *trey* of *yerts* weds new and old with allure

only then can i put myself
back into drive, and move
to the beat of this crazy jive

Elizabeth Robin retired to Hilton Head Island after a 33-year teaching career to devote herself to writing. *Silk Purses and Lemonade* (Finishing Line Press, 2017) is her first book. She found poetry in 2012 as a response and outlet to a fresh grief, watching her brother die from acute myeloid leukemia after 27 months of treatment.

Her second book, *Where Green Meets Blue* honors Robin's late husband. The title comes from a line in the poem "Whereafter," which chronicles a pivotal moment she transitioned from mourning all she had lost with his death in 2016, to embracing joyful memories of their married life. Those moments we make that purposeful choice, says Robin, we engage in possibility, and can live a more deliberate life.

A poet of witness and discovery, she relates both true and fictional stories about her Lowcountry present and world-traveling past. Writing offers her a lens to view the world, and a strategy to thrive within its madness. While many find faith carries them, Robin pins hope to compassion, sheer will, and the integrity in acceptance.

Her work appears in *The Fourth River, Foliate Oak Literary Magazine, I am not a silent poet, Autumn Sky Poetry Daily, Curly Mind, The Skinny Journal* and locally in *The Breeze* and the Island Writers' Network's *Time and Tide* (2015) and *Ebb and Flow* (2017). See more at www.elizabethrobin.com.